W9-ANH-531

Meeting Needs in our Community

Rachel Eagen

CRABTREE
PUBLISHING COMPANY
WWW.CRABTREEBOOKS.COM

Money $ense

An Introduction to Financial Literacy

Author: Rachel Eagen

Series research and development: Reagan Miller

Editors: Reagan Miller and Janine Deschenes

Design and photo research: Tammy McGarr

Proofreader: Petrice Custance

Prepress technician: Tammy McGarr

Print and production coordinator: Katherine Berti

Photographs
iStock: ©Steve Debenport, pp 12 (left), 21; ©andresr, p 14

Shutterstock: ©KingJC, p 2 (bottom middle); ©Sarine Arslanian, p 5 (bottom left); ©prosiaczeq, p 8 (right); ©Trong Nguyen, p 10; ©Sorbis, p 13; ©Tooykrub, p 18 (left)

All other images from Shutterstock

Library and Archives Canada Cataloguing in Publication

Eagen, Rachel, 1979-, author
    Meeting needs in our community / Rachel Eagen.

(Money sense : an introduction to financial literacy)
Includes index.
Issued in print and electronic formats.
ISBN 978-0-7787-5185-4 (hardcover).--
ISBN 978-0-7787-5187-8 (softcover).--
ISBN 978-1-4271-2137-0 (HTML)

    1. Economics--Juvenile literature. 2. Exchange--Juvenile literature. 3. Supply and demand--Juvenile literature. 4. Consumer goods--Juvenile literature. 5. Prices--Juvenile literature. I. Title.

HB183.E24 2018   j330   C2018-902968-4
                                     C2018-902969-2

Library of Congress Cataloging-in-Publication Data

Names: Eagen, Rachel, 1979- author.
Title: Meeting needs in our community / Rachel Eagen.
Description: New York : Crabtree Publishing Company, [2018] |
   Series: Money sense: An introduction to financial literacy |
   Includes index.
Identifiers: LCCN 2018025225 (print) | LCCN 2018034943 (ebook) |
   ISBN 9781427121370 (Electronic) |
   ISBN 9780778751854 (hardcover) |
   ISBN 9780778751878 (pbk.)
Subjects: LCSH: Business enterprises--Juvenile literature. |
   Customer services--Juvenile literature. | Selling--Juvenile literature.
   | Prices--Juvenile literature.
Classification: LCC HF5351 (ebook) | LCC HF5351 .E14 2018 (print) |
   DDC 338--dc23
LC record available at https://lccn.loc.gov/2018025225

Crabtree Publishing Company

www.crabtreebooks.com   1-800-387-7650

Printed in the U.S.A./092018/CG20180719

Published in Canada
Crabtree Publishing
616 Welland Ave.
St. Catharines, Ontario
L2M 5V6

Published in the United States
Crabtree Publishing
PMB 59051
350 Fifth Avenue, 59th Floor
New York, New York 10118

Published in the United Kingdom
Crabtree Publishing
Maritime House
Basin Road North, Hove
BN41 1WR

Published in Australia
Crabtree Publishing
3 Charles Street
Coburg North
VIC 3058

Table of Contents

Hi, I'm Ava and this is Finn. Get ready for an inside look on spending, saving, and more! The *Money Sense* series explores smart ways to think about and manage money.

After reading this book, join us online at Crabtree Plus to learn more and solve problems. Just use the Digital Code on page 22 in this book.

Buying the Things We Want and Need

It's normal to want things, such as a new bike or computer. But do you really need them? **Needs** are the things that every person must have to survive. Some of your needs are clothing, food, and a place to live. **Wants** are things you would like to have. What are some of your wants?

Sometimes it can be hard to tell the difference between wants and needs.

Goods and Services

We meet our needs and wants by using goods and services. Goods are things you can touch, such as a loaf of bread or a toothbrush. Services are things that others do for you, such as cutting your hair or fixing your car.

Most goods and services cost money. We give money to stores in **exchange** for goods. We give money to people in exchange for services.

Producers and Consumers

Producers might sew clothing, grow vegetables, or fix bicycles.

Producers are the people who make goods and provide services. **Consumers** are the people who buy goods and services. Everyone is a consumer. That's because all people buy goods and services to meet their wants and needs. But not everyone is a producer.

Make "**cents**" of it!

You are a consumer! For one day, make a list of all the goods and services you use. Here are some ideas to get you started.

- **Toothpaste and water**
- **Breakfast cereal and milk**
- **My clothing: a shirt, pants, socks, and shoes**
- **Books, computer, and pencil at school**

- **Music lessons**
- **Soccer coaching**
- **Dinner: chicken, vegetables, and pasta**

Goods and Services In My Community

Different communities produce different goods and services. The goods and services a community produces depends on things such as its **environment**, its location, and the people who live there.

A community that is near a famous **landmark**, such as Niagara Falls, might offer tour services to visitors.

People who live in areas with cold weather might make and sell warm scarves.

Foods grow best in certain environments. **Prairie** communities produce a lot of wheat.

We Need Producers

There are different kinds of producers in your community. They are important parts of your community because they make goods and provide services that allow you to meet your needs and wants. Most producers go to school or take part in training to learn the skills and knowledge they need to make goods and provide services.

Doctors spend many years being trained to provide people with health care.

Chefs and bakers learn how to make delicious foods at a school.

What is Scarcity?

Communities do not have an endless **supply** of goods and services. Supply is how much of something is available to buy or use. **Demand** is the amount of something that people want or need. **Scarcity** happens when the supply of a good or service is not large enough to meet the demand for it.

SORRY SOLD OUT!

Most communities cannot produce all of the goods and services required to meet all the people's wants and needs.

Strawberry Scarcity

In many communities, strawberries are grown only during warm months. The supply of strawberries is high in summer and low in winter. But if the demand for strawberries stays the same all year, there may be scarcity in winter when the supply is low. To help stop scarcity, grocery stores might buy strawberries from communities with warm **climates**, where they can be grown all year.

If strawberries are scarce in a community, consumers might have to buy different fruit.

Trade In My Community

Communities **trade** goods and services with each other. They bring in goods from other communities to meet the demand of consumers. A lot of trade happens within communities, too! Trade is the exchange of goods and services for money, or for other goods and services.

In the past, people exchanged goods and services for other goods and services. Today, people usually exchange money for goods and services.

When you buy a good or service, you are trading in your local market.

Your Local Market

Most people buy goods and services in a **market**. A market is any place where goods and services are bought and sold between producers and consumers. The exchange of goods and services in your community is your **local** market.

The Cost of Producing

It costs money to produce goods and services. Producers need to buy goods that help them make other goods and provide services. A hairdresser needs to buy scissors to cut hair. To make shoes, a shoe company needs to buy shoe materials, such as leather and glue. It also needs to buy machines to make the shoes.

A shoe company also needs to pay money to the workers who make the shoes.

Knowledge and Skills

Producers also need their own knowledge and skills to produce goods or services. Mechanics go to school to learn how to fix cars. Musicians practice their playing skills so that they can produce beautiful music. Building knowledge and skills takes time. Producers often pay money for education and training.

To produce food, farmers need knowledge and skills about how to grow it. They also need goods, such as tractors!

Selling Goods and Services

Producers sell the goods they make and the services they provide to earn an **income**. Producers can only earn an income if they sell their goods or services for more money than it cost to make the goods or provide the services.

Everyone needs an income to buy the things they need and want.

1/2 PRICE SALE

In any market, the same goods and services from different producers are usually sold for a similar amount of money.

How Much?

Price is the amount of money consumers pay for a good or service. Price depends on supply and demand. Goods and services with a low supply and high demand are harder to get. They usually have higher prices. Goods and services with a high supply are easier to get. They usually have lower prices.

What's the Price?

People make choices about the goods and services they buy based on price. People can't **afford** to buy everything they want, so they choose to buy goods and services with prices they can afford.

The same types of goods and services can have different prices. A **brand-name** T-shirt has a higher price than a T-shirt that is not brand-name. People have to make choices about which goods and services they buy.

JUST DO IT.

Many people make **budgets** to plan how they will spend money.

Make "**cents**" of it!

Make a list of the food items you need and want. Then visit a grocery store with a parent or caregiver. Write down the prices of each item on your list.

At home, rank the items from most to least expensive.

1. Which 3 items are the most expensive? Are they wants or needs?

2. Which 3 items are the least expensive? Are they wants or needs?

Imagine you are shopping for food. How do your buying choices depend on the price and type of item you want or need?

Part of Your Local Market

From growing food to giving music lessons, producers make goods and provide services that the people in their community need and want. Producers depend on consumers who choose to buy their goods and services. Think about how you are a consumer and a producer in your local market!

Producers and consumers depend on each other in their local market!

Make "cents" of it!

You can be a producer in your local market! You can sell a good or service that has demand. How about selling lemonade on a hot summer day? Here's what you will need:

- Lemonade
- Sign
- Cash box
- Jug or pitcher
- Cups
- Table and chairs

With the help of a grown-up, write down how much money it cost you to make one jug of lemonade. Write down the number of glasses that can be filled with one jug. Then decide on the price of one glass. To earn money, you need to sell the lemonade for more money than it cost to make it!

Most people are both producers and consumers in their communities!

Learning More

Books

Adler, David A. *Prices! Prices! Prices! Why They Go Up and Down.* Holiday House, 2015.

Bullard, Lisa. *Lily Learns about Wants and Needs.* Lerner Publishing Group, 2014.

Gill, Shelley. *The Big Buck Adventure.* Scholastic, 2002.

Websites

Learn more about how scarcity affects buying choices at the Social Studies for Kids website.
www.socialstudiesforkids. com/articles/economics/ scarcityandchoices1.htm

Try some fun financial games at The Mint: Fun for Kids.
www.themint.org/kids

For fun challenges, activities, and more, enter the code at the Crabtree Plus website below.

www.crabtreeplus.com/money-sense

Your code is:
ms06

22

Words to Know

Note: Some **boldfaced** words are defined where they appear in the book.

afford (*uh*-FAWRD) verb To have enough money to buy something

brand-name (BRAND-neym) adjective Describes a good, such as clothing, that is identified by a certain popular name, such as Nike

budgets (BUHJ-its) noun Plans for how money will be spent over a period of time

climate (KLAHY-mit) noun The usual weather in a place

environment (en-VAHY-r*uh* n-m*uh* nt) noun The natural surroundings in a place

exchange (iks-CHEYNJ) verb To give something for something else, usually money

income (IN-kuhm) noun Money received, or coming in, for work

landmark (LAND-mahrk) noun A natural or human-made object that is easily recognizable

local (LOH-kuh l) adjective Belonging or related to a specific area, such as a neighborhood or town

prairie (PRAIR-ee) noun A large, open area of land covered by grass

trade (treyd) verb The exchange of something for something else

A noun is a person, place, or thing.

A verb is an action word that tells you what someone or something does.

An adjective is a word that tells you what something is like.

23

Index

About the Author

Rachel Eagen is a writer and editor. She spends most of her free time baking cookies, listening to music, playing ukulele, and going on adventures with her son. Her happiest days are spent consuming books and chocolate-covered potato chips at the beach with her family.